HANG LENNY POPE

and

cloud:burst

Theatre Absolute, in co-production with Warwick Arts Centre, present

HANG LENNY POPE

Written and directed by Chris O'Connell

Cast

Lenny	Lee Colley
Ray	John Flitcroft
Caroline	Amanda Crossley
Mia	Rachel Brogan

Creative Team

Writer / Director	Chris O'Connell
Producer	Julia Negus
Original Soundscape	Andy Garbi
Set and Costume Design	Janet Vaughan
Lighting Design	James Farncombe
Dramaturg	John Ginman
Trainee Director	Lizzie Wiggs
Design Assistant	Emma Blundell
Company Stage Manager	Nicci Burton
Production Management	Mark Beasley for **next**stage solutions Ltd
Technical Support by	**next**stage solutions Ltd
Marketing and Press	Jill Cotton
	Chamberlain AMPR
	020 7240 5220
Print	Pixeltrix
Production Photographs	Manuel Harlan

Theatre Absolute
57–61 Corporation Street
Coventry
CV1 1GQ
024 7625 7380
info@theateabsolute.co.uk
www.theatreabsolute.co.uk

Registered Company No: 2966897

Coventry City Council

The first performance of *Hang Lenny Pope* took place on Monday 12 March 2007 at Warwick Arts Centre, Coventry.

UK Tour Spring 2007

Warwick Arts Centre, Coventry
12–17 March

Drum Theatre, Plymouth
20–24 March

The Point, Eastleigh
27–28 March

Corn Exchange, Newbury
29–30 March

mac, Birmingham
17–18 April

Lakeside Arts Centre, Nottingham
19–21 April

Northern Stage, Newcastle upon Tyne
24–28 April

Trinity Theatre, Tunbridge Wells
1–2 May

Tobacco Factory, Bristol
3–5 May

theatre **absolute**

Theatre Absolute is a multi award winning theatre company. Founded in 1992, and based in Coventry, its core members are Julia Negus, producer, and Chris O'Connell, artistic director and writer.

The company commissions, produces and tours new plays for the theatre that are bold, uncompromising and contemporary. Since 1999, they have earned a glowing reputation for their work, particularly through the making of *Street Trilogy (Car, Raw, Kid)* which thrilled audiences at the Edinburgh Festival, and toured both the UK and Europe to huge critical acclaim, and *cloud:burst*, which performed at the Firsts Festival, Royal Opera House, London, Tobacco Factory, Bristol and the Brits Off Broadway season, 59E59 Theatre, in New York City.

The company places an emphasis on story and character, explored through a robust performance style and a rhythmic and heightened text, which is underpinned by soundscapes that intensify the momentum of the narrative and the experience of the audience as the world of the play gathers around them.

Winners Edinburgh Fringe First 2001
Winners Edinburgh Fringe First 1999
Winners Time Out (London) Award 1999

Learning and access is of strong importance to the company, all performances are accompanied by an intensive programme of theatre workshops and activities with young people.

Absolute thanks to the following people for their support on *Hang Lenny Pope*:

Brian Bishop, Malcolm D. Browning, Louise Beckett, Paul Copley, Neil Darlison, Marion Doyen, Georgina Egan, Alison Gagen, Ana Gillespie, Rebecca Hannah, Graeme Hawley, Clare Huby, Jane Hytch, Richard Jordan, Kasseem Khuman, Paul Lucas, Lyric Hammersmith, Claire Maddocks, Rebekah Manning, Andy Moore, Ben O'Brien, Alan Rivett, Ashley Saville-Boss, Debbie and Ron Squires, Susan Twist, Nick 'Walks' Walker, Anna Western, Sheila and Terry O'Connell, Joe and Reuben.

Thanks also to Arts Council England, Coventry City Council, and Sir Barry Jackson Trust.

AN INTRODUCTION TO BOTH PLAYS

Hang Lenny Pope and *cloud:burst* were written in response to *Street Trilogy, (Car, Raw, Kid)* which was produced and toured by Theatre Absolute in 2005. The trilogy played for fifteen weeks in a host of British towns, with a cast of eleven actors playing sixteen characters. The whole thing, as fantastically well received as it was, felt so huge and so epic that it made me want to lie down in a darkened room! What has emerged for Theatre Absolute and for myself since then, has been a desire to strip things back and write almost for an empty stage.

The plays are linked by their connection to parenting, and loss. As the father of two young children, my gaze on the world has altered, largely in how I scan for danger in order to avoid it, devise advice and solutions, and by how I analyse the choices I make day to day regarding my kids. After writing *Street Trilogy*, which told the stories of young people whose parents where largely absent, it feels like a neat circle that the plays following should flip the coin, and tell stories from the perspective of parents.

Hang Lenny Pope unfolds over one evening in the Chapel of Rest in Brewer's Funeral Directors in a small, and once important, industrial town. Living in a city like Coventry, this is an element that resonates in a lot of my work; cities grow, but lives get left behind. Ray and Caroline,

mid-forties, have lost their son Lenny, a violent and tragic figure who has been killed by vigilantes. Through the toil of parenting him, they've also lost each other. This idea is linked to the loss of the child in *cloud:burst*; in most cases, it's the love between two people that creates a child. So when a new life arrives, where does the 'you and I' go? And when things start to go wrong in a family, what happens to that? Is it lost forever?

Hang Lenny Pope began as a question: are the parents to blame for the deeds perpetrated by their son Lenny? If he has murdered, caused unhappiness and exploited the weak for his own gain, how much can his mum and dad be held accountable? We're told we have choices. I worked in the probation service, and the mantra for offenders, and young offenders in particular, was often about choice; no one condemns you to a life of crime, you condemn yourself. And then I'd think, but do you? Where does your framework come from, the energy, the self-esteem that steers you, and burns inside? Isn't a child born empty, like a brand new MacBook waiting to be written, and created upon? How else is a child formed if not by its parents? Of course there's always consciousness and awareness, and a child is soon an adult and keen to make its own way, yet the residue of parenting, and the quality of a child's parenting, lies at the bottom of the glass.

These plays attempt to articulate my own personal feelings about the delicate art of rearing children, and the equally delicate truth that parents are human, often unsure, and at some point, always inexperienced. The plays are also a reaction to ongoing social hysteria about the well being of our children; they're not "like they used to be". If they're not, (which is open to debate) then there's a simple equation: we watch politicians appear routinely on television and tell lies. Some of us adopt their attitude as a route for life, some of us reject it. Children can do the same. And what do they make of the adult world as they look up to it? Are we comfortable with what they see?

In *cloud:burst*, I wanted to write about an extraordinary experience capturing and overwhelming a very ordinary person, which in turn explored ideas about the public ownership of traumatic events. I also wanted to explore 'aloneness'. The panic, and the fear, that in the claustrophobic atmosphere of a planet teeming with life, the only sound you can hear is yourself, taking in air, trying to stay calm. A one person play seemed the perfect vehicle to express this. Dominic is a man who has believed for most of his life that he doesn't really count, that nothing he does will ever change that. He's part of a mass psychological profile, an anonymous band of society, not rich, not poor, not good, not bad, just there. Breathing. And then his life is turned upside down, he becomes public property because of the bad deeds of others, and because the media have decided to put him there, they've decided it's his murdered child that's interesting, and not someone else's child murdered three weeks ago. Dominic has no idea if life can ever be normal again and yet when the media goes, as it does at the start of the play, he is essentially alone. And so what will this man do? How must he act? What should he believe?

For both plays, I express huge thanks to everyone who's been involved. Thanks in particular to Neil Darlison and Alan Rivett at Warwick Arts Centre, Coventry, for their belief in both pieces, (let's do it again!), and to Camilla Whitworth-Jones of the Helen Hamlyn Trust, for fostering and supporting *cloud:burst*.

Thanks also to Graeme Hawley for his courageous work in *cloud:burst*, up on the stage alone, Janet Vaughan and James Farncombe for the way they translate what I can only ever call "the atmosphere of the play", to Andy Garbi for sending shivers down my spine, to the actors in HLP for their fun, and for their conviction, to my two boys Joe and Rube, and to producer Julia Negus for her unswerving dedication to my words, and to Theatre Absolute.

Chris O'Connell
January 2007

CAST AND CREATIVE TEAM

Chris O'Connell
Writer / Director

Chris was writer-in-residence for Paines Plough, 1999-2000, and most recently was Playwright in Residence at Birmingham University, attached to their M(Phil) in playwriting, 2005-2006. Plays for Theatre Absolute include: *cloud:burst* (Royal Opera House, London 2005/ 59E59 Theatre, New York 2006), and *Car, Raw and Kid* (Edinburgh Festival, national and European tours, 1999-2003). *Car* and *Raw* won Fringe First Awards for Outstanding New Work and Innovation at the Edinburgh Fringe Festivals 1999 and 2001 respectively. *Car* won a Time Out Live Award for Best New Play on the London Fringe, 1999 and the three plays were performed together for the first time as *Street Trilogy*, and toured throughout the country in Spring 2005. Other work includes: *Tall Phoenix* (Belgrade Theatre), *Thyestes*, (RSC) *Hymns* (Frantic Assembly), *Hold Ya'* (Red Ladder Theatre Co), *Auto* (Vanemuine Theatre, Estonia), *Cool Water Murder* (Belgrade Theatre), *The Blue Zone* (mac Productions) and *Gabriel's Ashes* (BBC Radio 4). His work has been both read and produced in Estonia, Italy, Australia and America.

Julia Negus
Producer

Trained at Webber Douglas Academy of Dramatic Art, London, Julia co-founded Theatre Absolute in 1992 with writer Chris O'Connell. She has produced all of the company's work to date, including *Car* (Edinburgh Fringe First 1999, Time Out Award 1999, national and international tours 2000), *Raw* (Edinburgh Fringe First 2001 and national tour 2002), *Kid* (Edinburgh Festival 2003), *Street Trilogy*, (UK national tour 2005), *cloud:burst* (Firsts Festival, Royal Opera House, London 2005, Brits Off Broadway Season, New York 2006). Julia is also a textile artist and recently won the Volvo Art and Design Award 2005.

Andy Garbi
Soundscape

Channel 4 Ideasfactory Film Music Award winner 2004, PRS Foundation ATOM award winner 2005, Birmingham Conservatoire Masters Prize for excellence 2005. Andy Garbi's dark and emotive style has recently been featured on Classic FM's Chiller Cabinet show and Late Night Lisa with his latest album *The Sound of One*. He has also made headline appearances at festivals across Europe, including Glastonbury and has performed on the same bill as the Prodigy, Roni Size, Trans Global Underground and Jah Wobble. Andy has represented the UK for music that earned him a commendation from the Royal Netherlands Embassy and the Arts Council of England and has written, performed and musically directed for Birmingham Royal Ballet as well as leading contemporary dance groups, theatre and film. With playwright Chris O'Connell, Andy has

scored music for *Street Trilogy (Car, Raw, Kid), Bluezone, Tall* Phoenix and most recently *cloud:burst*.
www.andygarbi.com

James Farncombe
Lighting Design

Previously for Theatre Absolute: *Street Trilogy (Car, Raw and Kid)* and *cloud: burst*. Other credits include: *Three Sisters* and *Forward* (Birmingham Rep); *Crooked* and *I Like Mine with a Kiss* (The Bush, London); *Blonde Bombeshells of 1943, Nathan The Wise, Osama The Hero, A Single Act* and *The Maths Tutor* (Hampstead Theatre, London); *Blest Be The Tie* and *What's In The Cat* (Royal Court, London); *Improbable Fiction* (directed by Alan Ayckbourn), *Making Waves* and *Soap* (Stephen Joseph Theatre, Scarborough); *Blues For Mr Charlie* (Tricycle and Ipswich Wolsey); *A Funny Thing Happened on the Way to the Forum* and *Vincent in Brixton* (New Wolsey, Ipswich); *Beautiful Thing* (Nottingham Playhouse); *Dead Funny* and *Abigail's Party* (York Theatre Royal); *Sing Yer Heart Out for the Lads, Lord Of The Flies, The Twits* and *Bloodtide* (Pilot Theatre Company); *Accidental Death Of An Anarchist, A View From The Bridge, What the Butler Saw, The Hypochondriac, Dead Funny, Popcorn* and *Improbable Fiction* (The Octagon, Bolton); *To Kill A Mockingbird, Master Harold And The Boys, West Side Story, Death Of A Salesman, Peter Pan, The Witches, Plague Of Innocence* and *Unsuitable Girls* (Leicester Haymarket Theatre); *High Heel Parrotfish, Urban Afro Saxons* and *Funny Black Women On The Edge* (Theatre Royal, Stratford East); *Playboy Of The West Indies* (Tricycle and Nottingham Playhouse); *This Lime Tree Bower* (The Belgrade Coventry); *Hysteria* (Exeter Northcott); *Amy's View* (Salisbury Playhouse and Royal Theatre, Northampton); *Krapp's Last Tape* (Lakeside Arts, Nottingham); *The Blue Room* and *The Elephant Man* (Worcester Swan Theatre); *East Is East* and *A Women Of No Importance* (New Vic Theatre, Stoke); *Goldilocks* (Lyric Theatre, Hammersmith); *Private Fears in Public Places, Speed-the-Plow, A Day In The Death Of Joe Egg, The Price* and *Larkin With Women* (Manchester Library Theatre).

Janet Vaughan
Set and Costume Design

Janet trained in Theatre Design at Nottingham Trent Polytechnic. She is a visual artist and designer who has designed site-specific and touring film and theatre works and created installation artworks for unusual and digital spaces. Janet has achieved particular recognition for her work as one third of mixed media experimentalists Talking Birds and her design for Talking Birds' *Smoke, Mirrors & the Art of Escapology* formed part of the UK entry to the 1999 Prague Quadrennial. The main focus of Janet's theatre design is site specific performance, devised productions and new writing. Recent work includes designing a mobile aluminium whale as the auditorium for an intimate one-man show; and transforming an empty shop unit into a revolving restaurant. Janet has also designed touring shows for Theatre Absolute, the Birmingham Rep, Yellow Earth Theatre, Triangle and Talking Birds.

John Ginman
Dramaturg

John has directed more than 70 shows in various regional theatres, including extended periods at the Belgrade Coventry, the Worcester Swan, and Contact Theatre Manchester. His own stage works include an adaptation of Dostoievski's *The Idiot* (Worcester and Manchester), libretti for Noir, Gulliver and Science Fictions (The Opera Band), and numerous plays for children. He currently teaches at Goldsmiths in London, where he convenes the MA in Writing for Performance.

Lizzie Wiggs
Trainee Director

Recent credits include: *cloud:burst* (Theatre Absolute, 59E59 Theatre, NYC); *The Whale* , *Three Doctors* (Talking Birds); *Being Alive (*national tour, Book Communications*); Maret/ Sade (*Punchdrunk*); Chasing Ibsen* (Eugenie Productions); *Broken Glass*, *A View From The Bridge, Score, Little Malcolm and his Struggle against the Eunuchs (*The Octagon Theatre, Bolton); *Jermyn Street Theatre Gala,* (Criterion Theatre, London) *Who's Afraid of The Big Bad Book?* (Soho Theatre, London); *Bottle Universe,* (The Bush Theatre); *Romeo and Juliet, Nutcracker, Beauty and the Beast, La Fille Mal Gardee, Two Pigeons, Swan Lake,* (Birmingham Royal Ballet); *Kid , Street Trilogy,* (Theatre Absolute).

Emma Blundell
Design Assistant

After graduating from the University of Central England in 2005 with a degree in Theatrical Design, Emma's theatre work includes: *Un-Earth, Dido and Aeneus, You Strike the Woman, You Strike the Roc, The Journey* and *No Going Back* (Midlands Arts Centre), *Hypochondriac, Jack and the Beanstalk* (The Belgrade Theatre, Coventry), *Dial 'M' for Murder* (Crescent Theatre, Birmingham), *Climb Aboard* (Balsall Heath Playhouse) and recently Alfred Hitchcock's *Strangers on a Train* and *The Lion, The Witch and The Wardrobe* (Oldbury Repertory Theatre).

Nicci Burton
Company Stage Manager

Nicci graduated as a Stage Manager in 2002 at Rose Bruford Drama College and was awarded the 2006 Stage Management Association Individual Award for Excellence in Stage Management. Recent work includes Deputy Stage Manager for *Lord of the Flies* (Pilot Theatre Company), *The Merchant of Venice* (Creation Theatre Company) and *Journey to the River Sea* (Theatre Centre/Unicorn Theatre Company) and as Stage Manager on the *Johnny Thunder Stunt Show* (Legoland, Windsor).

Mark Beasley for nextstage solutions Ltd
Production Management
nextstage solutions provide production management and technical support solutions for theatre and events. Current clients include *Hang Lenny Pope* (Theatre Absolute), *Sing Yer Heart Out for the Lads* (Pilot Theatre) and *5 Guys Named Moe* (Hughes Productions). Since the company was formed in 2006 nextstage solutions has worked on a wide range of projects from Benedon Schools production of *Noah's Flood* that toured to two churches in Kent and then Rochester Cathedral to the National Youth Theatre's 2006 season which culminated with a performance in Trafalgar Square, London involving 2000 performers. nextstage solutions work with companies to develop their technical ability and promote a confident image to venues and clients.
www.nextstagesolutions.co.uk

Lee Colley
Lenny
Lee trained at Italia Conti. Theatre work includes Allan Felix in *Play It Again Sam* (The Landor Upstairs), Ross McManus/ Jamie in *Cracked* (UK Tour), Lollipop Guild/ Flying Monkey in *Wizard of Oz* (RSC), Vocalist in *Iris* (Queen Elizabeth Hall), Starkey in *Peter Pan* (Millfield Theatre), Sheriff in *Babes In The Woods* (The Landor Upstairs), Chorus in *Puss In Boots* (Belgrade Theatre), Jason in *Car* (Pleasance, Edinburgh, London, & Worcester Swan), Mile End Steve in *Closer To Heaven* (National Youth Theatre), Toby in *Happy Families* (Kings Head), Jason in *Car* and Lee in *Kid* (both *Street Trilogy* for Theatre Absolute). Television credits include *The Murder of Stephen Lawrence* (Granada), *Snakes and Ladders* (World Productions), *Chalk* (BBC), *Brasseye* (Talkback Productions), *Never Never* (Company Television), *Band of Brothers* (HBO Productions), *Happiness* (BBC), *Red Cap* (Stormy Pictures Ltd), *Serious And Organised* (Company Pictures), *Cambridge Spies* (BBC), *The Bill* (Thames), *Hiroshima* (BBC), and *Holby* (BBC). Film work includes *The Key* (Alomo Films), *Gulf Shadows* (Yorkshire Television), and *Categories of Happiness* (Panico Studios).

John Flitcroft
Ray
John's theatre credits include: Toad in *Wind in the Willows* (Theatre By The Lake, Keswick), *Of Mice and Men* (Birmingham Repertory Theatre and national tour), *The Shooky, Playland, Silence* and *Nativity* (Birmingham Repertory Theatre) The Emperor in *The Emperor's New Clothes* (Moving Hands Theatre Company), *The Daughter in Law, The Wizard of Oz, Neville's Island* (Octagon Theatre, Bolton), *Don Juan* (West Yorkshire Playhouse) *A Midsummer Night's Dream* (The Dukes, Lancaster), *Lucky Sods* and *Happy Jack* (The Coliseum Theatre, Oldham), *Phil and Jill and Jill and Phil* (The Swan Theatre, Worcester and The Coventry Belgrade), *A Winter's Tale* (Salisbury Playhouse.) John has had a long

association with Pentabus Theatre Company, productions for them include: *Missing/Crossing, Dancing with the Devil and Becca's Children*. On television John has appeared in; *The Courtroom* (Mersey Television), *Cold Feet, Cruel Earth* and *Butterfly Collectors* (Granada Television), *Dalziel & Pascoe, The League of Gentlemen* (BBC), *The Royal, Emmerdale* and *Heartbeat* (Yorkshire Television). John has a great many radio credits for BBC Radio 4 including: *What Is Missing From Your Life?, The Psychology Of Dangerous Roads* and *The Worcester Pilgrim*.

Amanda Crossley
Caroline

Amanda trained at the RSAMD in Glasgow, graduating with the comedy award. Theatre credits include: *Medea* (international tour), *Romeo and Juliet, The Winters Tale* and *Twelfth Night* (all for Theatre Babel Scotland). Also in theatre: *A Taste of Honey* (Northface Theatre Company), *A Love Story* and Alan Ayckbourne's *Confusions* (Tristan Bates Theatre). Film and TV credits include: *Secrets and Lies* and *Topsy Turvy* (Mike Leigh), *The Craig Ferguson Theory* (BBC Scotland), *Sloggers* (BBC) *Emmerdale* (Yorkshire TV) and most recently, *Hollyoaks* (Lime Productions).

Rachel Brogan
Mia

Rachel has a great passion for the theatre, previously appearing for Theatre Absolute as Lex in *Raw - Street Trilogy* tour 2005. Other theatre credits include *Dog Boy, Port* and *The Sanctuary Lamp* (Royal Exchange Theatre, Manchester). She has also performed on the Royal Court stage in *Redundant* and *What's in the Cat* which was co-produced by Contact Theatre, where Rachel also appeared in *Iron*. TV credits include *Doctors, Casualty, Twisted Tales* (BBC) and *Blue Murder* (Granada). She is an experienced radio performer with five BBC credits to her name. Also an award winning producer, Rachel became a partner of Working Girls Theatre Company in 2005, winning a Manchester Evening News award for their production of *Iron* by Rona Munro, with Rachel being nominated for Best Actress.

Warwick Arts Centre, driven by the imaginations and creativity of today's artists, maintains the enviable position of being one of the best multi-disciplinary arts spaces in the UK outside of London.

With a mission to place the contemporary arts firmly within the everyday life of our audiences and participants, Warwick Arts Centre's response to the landscape of UK theatre has become ever more distinctive in recent years. With two theatre spaces with audience capacities of 550 and 140, our commitment is threefold: to support theatre companies, writers, actors, directors and producers living and working in the locality to realise their ambitions to create and tour vital and engaging theatre; to support the creation of new and emerging forms of theatre by companies and theatre makers across the UK; to present a programme of the best international theatre available to our audiences.

Warwick Arts Centre has maintained a long association with Theatre Absolute. In 2005 we embarked upon a major collaboration to produce and tour the award winning trilogy of plays written by Chris O'Connell, *Car, Raw* and *Kid* under the banner, *Street Trilogy*. At the same time we commissioned a new play by Chris O'Connell *cloud:burst*.

Hang Lenny Pope is our third collaborative adventure pairing the energetic Theatre Absolute with the driving force of Warwick Arts Centre.

Alan Rivett

Neil Darlison

Director

Deputy Director

Recent Commissions and Co-productions

The World in Pictures	Forced Entertainment
St George and the Dragon	Schtanhaus – Beggarsbelief
Thatcher The Musical!	Foursight Theatre
Saints and Superheroes	Flywheel Productions
cloud:burst	Theatre Absolute
Red Ladies	Clod Ensemble
25/7	Talking Birds
Jason and the Argonauts	Schtanhaus - Beggarsbelief
Ether Frolics	Shunt/Sound & Fury
The Race	Gecko Theatre
The Night Shift	Mark Murphy
Ghost Train	Marissa Carnesky
Street Trilogy	Theatre Absolute
A Christmas Carol	Wee Stories
An Audience with Mr Ritzy	Talking Birds

Chris O'Connell

HANG LENNY POPE

and

cloud:burst

OBERON BOOKS
LONDON

First published in 2007 by Oberon Books Ltd
521 Caledonian Road, London N7 9RH
Tel: 020 7607 3637 / Fax: 020 7607 3629
e-mail: info@oberonbooks.com
www.oberonbooks.com

A catalogue record for this book is available from the British Library.

Cover design: Pixeltrix

ISBN: 1 84002 733 9 / 978 1 84002 733 4

Printed in Great Britain by Antony Rowe Ltd, Chippenham

For three musketeers:

Jeremy Weller
John Ginman
Mark Babych

*all of whom have inspired and
supported me along the way.*

Contents

HANG LENNY POPE

Characters

RAY, 46

CAROLINE, 44

LENNY, their son, 24

MIA, Lenny's girlfriend, 19

Winter, the present day

Notes on the text:

A slash '/' indicates the point at which the next character starts speaking.

Words in italics signify emphasis rather than volume

Conversations between Lenny and Ray appear in lower case.

A chapel of rest in Brewers Funeral Directors.

There are two doors. One, stage right, is a pass door, and connects to the front reception of the premises. It is the door relatives would come through to view their recently deceased. The other door, stage left, is a door that leads to the yard and workshop behind the premises.

It is evening, not long after six o'clock. In the room is a coffin, containing the dead body of Lenny Pope.

Music plays.

As the lights rise, RAY is standing beside the coffin. Holding his hammer, he takes a finish nail from the palm of his hand, and lines it up, ready to tack it into the wood.

The music stops.

LENNY speaks from the coffin.

LENNY: six shiny nails sweating in his palm, and fucking
    hammer man's finishing the coffin, yeah?

RAY: wha /…?

LENNY: wriggling fucking fingers, / arching arm, anticipating.

RAY: what…?

LENNY: all day long dad, yeah? easy elbow extended, and you
    released it, dad, yeah? blood red brain, made the motion,
    swing, crack, thud, throbbing weight of the hammer, thud,
    thud, thud.

RAY: no.

LENNY: yeah. and how many nails in the coffin dad? and
    how many screws, do you think? how many nails and
    how many screws has ray, the coffin maker, used? lining
    up the nail, wriggling your fingers, i *love* that thing you do

with your fingers! and crack! just that bit there, dad, yeah? reach, grab, crack! reach, grab, crack! reach, grab, crack! reach, grab, crack! (*Beat.*) and then you're done dad. yeah?

RAY: yeah.

LENNY: so now smash it up.

RAY: wha…?

LENNY: smash it up.

RAY: what…?

LENNY: *smash it up!!!*

RAY: what…?

LENNY: the coffin.

RAY: the coffin?

LENNY: the coffin.

RAY: the coffin?

LENNY: my coffin.

RAY: your coffin?

LENNY: *yeah, smash the fucking thing up dad!!!*

RAY: smash…? no. *no.*

LENNY: yes, yes.

RAY: no, cos you're, cos you…

LENNY: I know. and so that's why I'm asking you, smash it dad, smash it. (*Deliberate.*) *just-fucking-smash it!!!*

RAY: *lenny*

LENNY: it's me going down to the black, when you walk out that door. 1,2,3,4, is this what you became a coffin maker for?

A sudden silence.

RAY walks a few tentative steps towards the coffin, and lifts the lid off. LENNY sits bolt up right.

Raaaaaaaaa!!

RAY: FUCK!!!!! get out!!…get out! what the fuck's…?!!…*get out!!*

CAROLINE enters from the yard door. RAY sees her. He stops.

Alright?

Beat.

CAROLINE: What're you doing?

RAY: What?

CAROLINE: What're you…?

RAY: Nothing. I…

CAROLINE: Can I come in?

RAY: Of course you can.

She shakes out her brolly.

CAROLINE: What?

RAY: Eh?

CAROLINE: Staring at me.

RAY: I wasn't, I…

CAROLINE: (*Irritated.*) You're in a trance.

RAY: Am I? Sorry.

CAROLINE: Girl in the office said you were in the workshop. (*Gestures to the workshop beyond.*) I was on my way over…

RAY: Yeah, no, I'm in here, I've just finished the lid. It's not the best I've ever made. The lads got him out the cold room, laid him in. Do you want to see him?

CAROLINE looks at the coffin, realising it's LENNY.

27

I've just finished.

CAROLINE: I wasn't expecting to see him.

RAY: He'll still be here in the morning, if you want to come
back down.

CAROLINE: Yeah.

RAY: Or come and see him now. It's okay. Just don't…

CAROLINE: Don't what?

RAY: Don't worry what he looks like. He's still a mess, but he
looks tidier. He's been embalmed.

*RAY puts a hand out, gestures CAROLINE over. She moves slowly
towards the coffin, stops at its side, and looks in. She turns away
dismissively.*

CAROLINE: Huh.

RAY: Caz.

Silence.

(*Nodding towards the girl in the office.*) Is she still working?

CAROLINE: Just finished. She said don't forget to lock the pass
door.

RAY: Right.

Silence.

So what you been doing? How you feeling? You haven't sat
in the house all day, eh? I rang you.

CAROLINE: Been clearing his stuff.

RAY: Clearing his…? / He's hardly…

CAROLINE: Ten days. How long do we wait? (*Soft.*) Nothing's
chucked, there's a couple of bin bags, you can have a look
when you get home, see what you think.

RAY: You didn't hear the phone then?

CAROLINE: Depends when you rang. I went out. I took some flowers down to where the girl died, there was a lot there, tied to the railings, teddies, scarves.

RAY: Right.

CAROLINE: And I dropped into the shop. They asked about you,

RAY: Yeah?

CAROLINE: There's a sale on, big rush for wellies. 'How's Ray taking it?' One of the girls said I've got that look again, now Lenny's died. I'm more like I was, before I met you. She said if she didn't know me she wouldn't believe I'm a mum.

RAY: Well you are.

CAROLINE: Was.

RAY: What is this?

CAROLINE: What?

RAY: *Go out and come back in again, eh?*

CAROLINE: You asked me what I did, *I was telling you.*

An exasperated silence. CAROLINE takes some sandwiches from her bag.

I made you these.

RAY: …

CAROLINE: Don't look so surprised. Something to do Ray, it's…

He inspects the sandwiches.

What did you ring me for?

RAY: See how you were. It was a courtesy call.

CAROLINE: Bloody call centre Ray.

RAY: Yeah.

They smile.

It does sound a bit… (*Shrugs.*) Just, me down here, you up there.

Silence.

CAROLINE: I wanted to talk.

RAY: What about?

CAROLINE: Can we go somewhere else?

RAY: I'm working.

CAROLINE: On what, it's finished isn't it?

RAY: (*Of the coffin.*) I'm going to start it again.

CAROLINE: For God's sake.

RAY: *What?…* You're as bad as her out there.

CAROLINE: Who?

RAY: People coming through here, Brewer makes sure they get what they want. Our boy dies, he offers to buy one in and her in the office…

CAROLINE: What?

RAY: This morning, she's smirking, acting like I'm a freak cos I'm making my own son's coffin. I've made the coffins here for the last twenty years. It makes sense I make Lenny's. It's what I want. What's wrong with that? I told Brewer. 'I'll lock up, I'm not going till the coffin's right. I'll be here all night if I have to.' It's my last one Caz. With the closure. It's the last one I'll make, and it's Lenny's. It needs to be right.

Silence. RAY rubs his eyes.

CAROLINE: Look knackered.

RAY: Can't sleep.

CAROLINE: Calm down a bit.

RAY: Yeah.

CAROLINE: What do you mean, closure?

RAY: A firm. I'm not sure who they are. They're buying the land, they're building a gym. It's like a members club.

CAROLINE: Since when?

RAY: Last week, week before last.

CAROLINE: First I've heard.

RAY: It's been a bit… (*Pointed; meaning Lenny's death.*) You know? (*Easier.*) According to Brewer, it's… I'm (*Sarcastic Brewer voice.*) 'part of a dying breed'. / Like I'm some…

CAROLINE: You're forty-six.

RAY: I know. But he's done it. I said to him, 'You can't just finish me' And he's like, (*Brewer's voice.*) 'Town's changed Ray, doesn't need people like you any more, in two years' time they'll have people commuting from London.'… He'll die rich. I told him, 'You're a prick, you can't just walk all over me…'

She smiles, wry.

What?

CAROLINE: You.

RAY: Me?

CAROLINE: If you'd thought like that twenty-five years ago we wouldn't be in the mess we are now.

RAY: How'd you work that one out?

CAROLINE: Wouldn't be sat here for a start.

31

RAY gets his hammer and sorts some nails into his hand, continuing to tack them along the rim of the lid as they talk.

RAY: (*Wry.*) No, well that's cos we'd be wanderers. Trekking down the Amazon.

CAROLINE: What?

RAY: Catching trains. Where was it?

CAROLINE: What?

RAY: Trains, boats. Can't just go swanning off Caz…

CAROLINE: Why can't you?

RAY: You came down here to talk about trains.

CAROLINE: No.

RAY: Hollywood, the other side of the world.

CAROLINE: Not important where, just that we went Ray.

RAY: Right.

CAROLINE: That people knew we did it.

RAY: Yeah, well twenty-five years ago I was working down here, twenty-five years ago you didn't just walk away from a job.

CAROLINE: No.

RAY: A bunch of animals battered our kid to death with two baseball bats, and an iron bar. Caz. I don't really give a fuck to be honest. Right now, all I want to do is get Len's coffin right, and after that Brewer can stick his job up his arse.

Long silence.

CAROLINE: What's he been saying anyway?

RAY shrugs.

Local leper this morning.

RAY looks at CAROLINE.

Bus driver's staring at me, he knows who I am, but he doesn't say anything, just that look, you know? Girl in the newsagent on the Quadrant, she refused to serve me; a packet of Extras and she tells me to fuck off.

RAY turns back in from the door.

You can see what people are thinking. Like they're all bloody perfect.

He sits.

Maybe I'll stay at home, close the curtains, hang my head in shame.

Silence

Ray.

RAY: What?

CAROLINE: *Talk to me for Christ's sake.*

RAY: I don't know what to say, close the curtains, why? I don't give a shit.

CAROLINE: I do, *I* give a shit.

RAY: I know you do.

CAROLINE: That's why I've broke my back making sure that kid knows what's right and what's wrong.

RAY: Yeah.

CAROLINE: *So how did he get to murder someone?*

RAY: I don't know.

CAROLINE: The Big fucking I Am, pushing his drugs, his... Scarecrow bloody hoodies from across the estate, lives ruined because he couldn't find any respect for another human being. Why couldn't he? (*Gestures outside.*) That's why they're all at it, and that's why Brewer's dumped you, ask him. Lenny killed that girl, and everyone blames us. They blame his parents.

Beat.

Ray.

Beat.

RAY: Yeah.

Beat.

Just.

Beat

Do you want this sandwich?

CAROLINE: *Fuck off!!!!*

CAROLINE grabs the remaining sandwich and squashes it up, chucking it to the floor.

Fucking cheese and pickle / on the floor Ray!!... and fucking Lenny Pope's bad...

RAY: Calm down.

CAROLINE: Everyone knows what he did... *'Hang Lenny Pope',* I saw it written on a wall... (*She goes to the coffin.*) You're famous now mate, never enough for you just being someone's son, you're a celebrity now, all over the papers, us too... You got us all over the papers... You...

She sits, weeping.

Tell me you didn't do it.

She weeps.

What was going through your head?

Long silence. CAROLINE takes RAY's hand, she holds it. She kisses his hand, keeping her lips on it. She stands and pulls him to her.

She starts to kiss him, vulnerable, wanting him. He responds and they kiss. We hear LENNY from the coffin.

LENNY: oi! dirty bastard!

RAY keeps on kissing.

eh! you dirty bastard!

They continue kissing.

I SAID, EH! YOU DIRTY FUCKING BASTARD…

RAY pulls away.

CAROLINE: What's wrong?

LENNY: give us a quid, and i'll piss off for half an hour.

RAY: (*To CAROLINE.*) Nothing.

LENNY: might be too long.

CAROLINE: Ray.

LENNY: make it twenty.

RAY: (*To CAROLINE.*) We shouldn't.

LENNY: make it ten. ten minutes, and hope for the best!

CAROLINE heads for the door that leads out to the yard.

RAY: Where you going?

CAROLINE: *Get some air… I don't know, just…*

RAY: I thought you wanted to talk.

She stops at the door, looking outside. She breathes.

CAROLINE: I'm going down to the garage. I need some fags…

RAY: Right.

She goes. RAY watches her, checks his pockets.

(*Calls.*) I could do with some myself. (*Beat.*) If you're going...

No answer. He watches CAROLINE *some more, and then steps back into the Chapel of Rest.*

LENNY: you got rid of her then?

RAY: she's gone to the garage.

LENNY: where were we?

RAY: what?

LENNY: i've been ever so patient listening to you two. right laugh you two, yeah dad?

RAY: there's a lot to talk about.

LENNY: you mean me?

RAY: it's always you, you know that. len / listen, i'm not really...

LENNY: bit shit, don't you think? comes down here, and all she's bothered about is you two getting it on.

RAY: leave it.

LENNY: thought your boat was coming in dad, yeah?!! (*Shudders.*) the idea of your parents shagging, it's too much for any kid, but not while i'm lying / here, not while...

RAY: i've got to get on.

LENNY: save yourself the bother, and come here.

RAY: what?

LENNY: come here.

RAY moves to the coffin.

closer.

RAY moves closer.

i want to make a pact.

RAY: eh?

LENNY: grab your hammer, smash the thing up, and we'll fuck
off down the pub dad, yeah?

RAY: (*Laughs.*)

LENNY: i'm serious, smash the thing up and hand in your
badge dad, yeah? can't stand enclosed spaces at the best of
times, so why waste the night fussing?

RAY: because / you're…

LENNY: because i'm what?

RAY: you've got to have a coffin.

LENNY: why?

RAY: you died.

> *Beat*

LENNY: so lift off the lid. let the light into your dead boy's
eyes.

> *RAY lifts the lid off. LENNY sits up.*

> (*Nods hello.*) dad.

> *Beat.*

RAY: (*Nods hello back.*) len.

LENNY: sorry about earlier. didn't mean to shit you up.

RAY: right.

LENNY: (*Inspecting the quality of the coffin.*) can see why you've
been worrying.

RAY: i was hoping you wouldn't notice.

LENNY: got a question.

RAY: what?

LENNY: you having me cremated dad, yeah?

RAY: yeah.

LENNY: nice one. so then you won't be needing the lid, am i right?

RAY: how'd you work that one out?

LENNY: furnace, not like burial, not like keeping the worms out.

RAY: all coffins have lids len.

LENNY: why all dad, why *all?* and why in particular when you're going to be cremated?

RAY: (*Laughs.*) superstition, more wood for the flames to lick at? i don't know, / never thought about it that deeply.

LENNY: so if you don't know *why* you need a lid, why have you made *me* a lid?

RAY sighs.

which leads me to this. if you won't go down the no coffin route, then i'm prepared to compromise. the pact, with some adjustment, can go like this: coffin maker makes the coffin, but coffin maker doesn't make the lid.

RAY: no.

LENNY: no?

RAY: no way.

LENNY: instead. yeah?

RAY: can't not make the lid.

LENNY: it's my only chance.

RAY: can't.

LENNY: says who?

RAY: (*Shrugs.*)

LENNY: rule book?

RAY: no.

LENNY: so who?

RAY: can't not make the lid. it's not done len.

LENNY: try it.

RAY: can't. (*Looks at the lid.*) i've already done it.

LENNY: so we'll trash it.

RAY: can't.

LENNY: try.

RAY: can't.

LENNY: can't is can's brother.

RAY: can is can't's younger *foolish* brother.

LENNY: rule books stink.

RAY: nothing to do with rule books. obvious.

LENNY: the way of things?

RAY: yeah.

LENNY: there has to be a lid?

RAY: yeah.

LENNY: always?

RAY: yeah.

LENNY: rule books then.

RAY: no.

LENNY: *is*.

RAY: isn't.

LENNY: isn't is is's brother.

RAY: that's easy for you to say?!

LENNY: Bu bum!

RAY: (*Northern comedian voice.*) 'i'm here all week.'

They laugh.

LENNY: roll up, roll up. new ways dad, yeah? no lid.

RAY: got to have a lid.

LENNY: (*Scouse voice.*) are you starting again?

RAY: (*Scouse voice.*) are you dancing?

LENNY: (*Scouse voice.*) are you asking?

RAY: 'computer says no.'

LENNY: 'yeah but, no but.'

They laugh.

dad!!! (*Deliberately.*) no-lid, we'll chuck that one away, and tonight, under the cover of darkness, lenny pope rises, glasses, wig...

RAY: eh?

LENNY: for disguises. (*American voice of officialdom.*) 'Houston, we have an escaped corpse on our hands' (*American siren noise.*) woo, woo, woo woo!!

RAY: you died.

LENNY: and you're there, by my side. we're in the car, feds in the rear view, and i'm disguised. i'm a sight. i'm a joke. i asked you to get me a wig, and it's an afro. it's an *AFRO* fucking wig dad, yeah?!

RAY: why would i / get you an...

LENNY: that's exactly what i'm thinking!

RAY: i don't understand.

LENNY: it's one of our scenarios. keep up.

RAY: i'm trying.

LENNY: and I'm lenny.

RAY: pleased to meet you.

LENNY: bu bum!

RAY: len…

LENNY: cool. so. you're there, with me, for the thrill. yeah? you, me, and my afro. and we drive, and we rob, and we laugh, and we steal, and we kill. dad. yeah?

Beat.

RAY: (*Cautious.*) kill who?

LENNY: anyone. someone. (*Ironic.*) i'm a murderer now, you know what people are saying.

RAY: len, whatever this is…

LENNY: it's the afterlife.

RAY: you need to leave me and your mum in peace.

LENNY: i'm the one with R.I.P. after his name.

LENNY stands up in the coffin. RAY stares up at him.

RAY: (*To himself.*) stop it.

LENNY: dad.

RAY: (*To himself.*) stop it.

LENNY: *i just want to talk.* that's the only reason i'm here.

RAY: got no time son, going to build / the whole thing again, you said it yourself, it's not…

LENNY: *listen to me for fuck's sake!*

RAY: you better calm down sunshine.

LENNY: piss off...

RAY: here we go.

LENNY: *those wankers with the baseball bats!* dad. the bastards that killed me, they hit me too soon. okay? i wanted to talk to them. i was putting my hands up dad. like this. (*His hands go up.*) yeah dad? slowly. because i didn't have nothing to hide.

Suddenly LENNY rugby-tackles RAY to the floor.

and then fucking WHACK!

RAY: watch my bloody knee, eh?!

LENNY: pack of wolves, they took me down dad. i'm telling myself: 'fist, nose, hit them in the solar plexus'. didn't you tell me about the solar plexus? and i'm down dad, i'm hit from behind, and i hiss, and i wish, and the world's a hurricane dad, yeah? it's not right.

RAY: let me up.

LENNY: it's not fair. they want justice. *i* want justice.

RAY: you should've thought about that before you decided to...get off, will you?

LENNY: why's everyone say i'm so bad, when *they* do what they did to me?

RAY: you-killed-their-sister.

LENNY: no-i-didn't. she *fell*, dad. we were on the roundabout, she was screaming, she pulled back. there was traffic for fuck's sake. i reached, and she pulled, and she fell. i've got the scratches. i reached to get her, i was too late, and the car hit her dad, yeah? but *fuck, no!!*... these men, these *apes*, they say i did it on purpose dad, yeah? fucking apes, her brothers, hunting me down with iron bars, dad. *apes* dad!! i'm not saying i wasn't there when she died, but did i torture, did i disfigure the beautiful girl??

RAY: no.

LENNY: say it.

RAY: *no.*

LENNY: no. i just wanted to make her see. i didn't kill her.
(*Beat.*) so why's everyone treat me so bad? (*Beat.*) dad?

RAY grabs the coffin lid.

RAY: lenny, no one cares whether you did it, or you didn't. the
girl's dead, and it's because of you, alright?

LENNY: so that's it? end of.

RAY: i need to get on.

LENNY: what was it we did, saturdays?

RAY: i don't know.

LENNY: don't pretend like we can't have this conversation.

RAY: we can't.

LENNY: so you're dreaming?

RAY: i don't know…

LENNY: what was it we did?

RAY: saturdays?

LENNY: yeah.

Beat.

RAY: we came down the yard. lazy saturdays in dad's
workshop. your mum'd bring down a flask, she left it
outside.

LENNY: since i was six, we've been in that workshop dad,
yeah? some days i'd wonder: why does he love that coffin
so much? cutting, planing, sweating, under your arms,
sweat, on your lip. cutting, planing. cutting, planing. how
long does it take to plane a piece of wood?

43

RAY: it's my job.

LENNY: and that way you steamed the wood dad. real oak, it came from a tree. 'Dad's making coffins...

RAY: ... to put away the dead.'

LENNY: that was it. and you make them strong dad, yeah?

RAY: gotta be strong. take the weight.

LENNY: and the dead dad, the dead don't come out again?

RAY: no.

LENNY: no second chances?

RAY shakes his head.

since i was six i've known this.

RAY: what're you saying to me len?

LENNY: you put that lid on, you let them burn me, and all i am, everything they say i am, it can't never be changed dad, yeah?

RAY hugs LENNY. He holds him. Tighter. Tighter.

RAY: are you big? *are you a big fucking man?*

LENNY shakes his head.

(*Vicious.*) no.

RAY composes himself; he tidies the collar on LENNY's jacket, combs LENNY's hair.

tell you the truth, i'm surprised you lasted as long you did. menacing the town the way you did.

LENNY: i thought you'd be impressed.

RAY: not really.

LENNY: you didn't stop me though.

RAY: like how exactly?

LENNY: wag your finger, ten minutes later we're mates again.

RAY: your mum's the one did the disciplining, you know she did. (*Flippant.*) we played to our strengths.

LENNY: 'cept you never spoke to each other.

RAY: meal times.

LENNY: 'pass the pepper, pass the salt.'

RAY: modern marriage, what you on about?

LENNY: (*Bats away RAY's combing.*) stop fussing.

RAY: queen said she'd drop in.

LENNY: (*Headline.*) 'queen meets pope.'

RAY: doesn't come much bigger than that.

LENNY: mia used to say to me, 'you're a pope, and if you're a pope that means you can do whatever you want.'

RAY: within reason.

LENNY: did you like her dad, yeah?

RAY: of course i did. i can't stop thinking about it.

LENNY: about what?

RAY: the girl. i could've…she came here to meet you. if i'd taken you home…

LENNY: if.

RAY: if i'd…

MIA: Hiya.

RAY looks to the pass door, and MIA stands there, framed by the light. It is twelve days previously.

RAY: i… gorgeous len. she was so…

The lights change.

Hi.

MIA: I'm looking for Lenny, the woman in the office said he was in here.

RAY: He went out.

MIA: Right.

She waits.

RAY: Are you alright? What's your name?

MIA: Mia.

RAY: Oh, right, *the* Mia. He's told me all about you.

MIA: Yeah?

RAY: He just nipped out to get some fags.

MIA: Can I wait?

RAY: Wait all you want, the lazy git'll take forever.

Beat.

MIA: (*Of the coffin.*) Is there anyone in there?

RAY: No.

MIA: You make the coffins.

RAY: Yeah.

MIA: Len says you're a craftsman.

RAY laughs.

Aren't you?

RAY: I try, I learnt it from my old man. I do a bit of everything to be honest, coffins, maintenance. I'm testing the wheels on this. (*He indicates the trolley mechanism the coffin is mounted on.*) Been squeaking. Days like today, we're wheeling them in and out, 'rellies' waiting in reception, can't have any

46

squeaking. (*He swings the coffin round, listening to the wheels.*)
Not doing it now.

They smile.

MIA: Len talks about you a lot.

RAY: He talks, I know that. Come in.

She steps further into the room.

How'd you know him?

MIA: School. He used to sell weed outside the gates… I was in
year ten.

RAY: Right.

MIA: I'm nineteen now, I mean I've…

RAY: You've grown up.

MIA: And then Lenny pushed in ahead of someone in the
salon.

RAY: Is that where you work?

MIA: Did. 'Cut Above The Rest'. Like a Saturday job, washing
hair… I hadn't seen him for a year and I was like… 'That's
Lenny Pope.'

RAY: And you washed Len's hair.

MIA: (*Smiles.*)

RAY: Romance today.

MIA: He wanted three rinses with conditioner, and a head
massage. Then he went upstairs on the sunbed. When's he
going to be back?

RAY: Shouldn't be long.

Pause.

How long've you been seeing him?

MIA: Five months. You're quite sarky. About Len.

RAY: You have to watch my son sweetheart.

MIA: I am.

RAY: He can be a nasty piece of work.

MIA: I know.

RAY: But that impresses you anyway.

MIA: Sorry, have I annoyed you? It's not like I don't know, he's told me about being in prison and stuff... /

RAY: Young offenders mainly. And *then* prison. He's proud of the prison.

MIA: Is he? I know what people think. Maybe I'm wrong, I don't know, it's just a feeling, like he'll put it all... If he thinks it's worth his while, if I can love him the way he needs to be loved.

RAY: He's never been unloved.

MIA: I know. I didn't mean it like that... I sound a bit...

RAY: A bit, yeah.

MIA's mobile rings. She answers it. RAY watches her.

MIA: (*Phone.*) Hiya... Nothing. Town. I'm waiting for someone. Just... Yeah. I'm not. *Dad*, I'm not. Alright?... Look, I'm going. Okay. You too... See you.

She hangs up.

RAY: Mia. What's that short for?

Beat.

MIA: It isn't.

LENNY enters with the cigarettes. He wears a different jacket to the real time scene.

LENNY: (*To RAY.*) Alright? Got your cigs.

RAY: Ta.

LENNY: (*Looks to MIA.*) Alright?

MIA: Hiya.

RAY: (*To LENNY.*) Change.

> *LENNY digs in his pocket. RAY inspects LENNY's hair.*

You could do with some conditioner on that. (*Camp.*) Oh, and don't forget the head massage.

LENNY: What?

RAY: We were having a chat, weren't we Mia?

MIA: Sorry.

LENNY: It's called style dad, you want to try it some time.

> *They laugh. CAROLINE appears at the door that leads to the yard; she has her brolly, but wears a different coat to the real time scene. She has a plaster over her cheek.*

> *An awkward pause.*

RAY: (*To CAROLINE.*) Alright?

LENNY: (*To MIA.*) Have you met my mum?

CAROLINE: (*To MIA.*) Do you want to wait outside love?

LENNY: (*To MIA.*) You're okay.

CAROLINE: (*To MIA.*) It's private.

LENNY: (*To MIA.*) Ignore her.

MIA: (*To CAROLINE.*) It's alright.

LENNY: *Mi…*

> *She pulls LENNY's cigarettes from his jacket pocket.*

MIA: I'll have a ciggie.

MIA steps outside the door. In contrast to earlier in the play, CAROLINE's energy is weaker, less vibrant, offering less protection.

LENNY: Got your text. Ta for that.

CAROLINE: I was waiting for you.

LENNY: Been helping dad.

CAROLINE: (*To RAY.*) I thought you were coming back to fix the window.

RAY: I am.

CAROLINE: Can't sit there with the bloody street staring in at us.

LENNY: They love a scene.

RAY: How's your face?

LENNY: Be alright if you'd listened to me. Told you before didn't I? Let dad deal with things. You've never given a fuck about me, so you don't need to get involved, you know what I'm saying?

CAROLINE: You're out of control.

LENNY: Fuck off.

CAROLINE: What?

LENNY: Fuck. Off.

CAROLINE: (*She looks to RAY.*) Tell him.

RAY: I have.

CAROLINE: Tell him again.

RAY: I have. He knows he's a prat, / I can't…lobotomise him, I can't…

CAROLINE: Can't what? You can't be bothered? All his life you've turned him against me and now you don't know if you're coming / or going.

RAY: Caz.

CAROLINE: He's got you wrapped round his little finger, he's sat there in the middle playing the two of us against each other and you're just… There's things I won't turn a blind eye to, you know that. (*To LENNY.*) You went too far Len, last night…

LENNY: I'm sorry about your face.

CAROLINE: Not just me… The brick through the window, people targeting us because of what *you're* doing. If / you think that's…

RAY: He doesn't.

She stops.

CAROLINE: I didn't come down to argue.

LENNY: What were you texting me for?

CAROLINE: To see you.

She goes to LENNY.

To tell you about the nightmares…

LENNY: What nightmares?

CAROLINE: I'm waking up…and I can feel something, it's coming Len, it's…

LENNY: What is?

CAROLINE: That's why I got so upset last night.

LENNY: Cos you're having nightmares?

CAROLINE: Because you're pushing things too far.

LENNY: You said you didn't / come to argue.

CAROLINE: I haven't. But you swagger round, you're stubbing out your cigarettes on that boy's / hands...

LENNY: He was a Goth mum, get real.

CAROLINE: You're hanging out with underage girls.

RAY: Nothing went on, / the police accepted that...

CAROLINE: But he's not stupid. (*To LENNY.*) Look at you. Treat me like I'm the villain, go on, you can't help yourself. But I'm just...

LENNY: You've come to warn me.

CAROLINE: I'm...

LENNY: There's an axe man out there coming my way, and you've come down to warn me. Cheers, / I'll look out for him.

CAROLINE: *I won't stand and watch...* What goes around Len. I want you to be my boy. All I want is the best for you, you know I do. And I want a chance.

RAY: For what?

CAROLINE: For us all to make a choice.

LENNY: About what?

CAROLINE: *This...* Last night...the whole bloody shambles of the three of us always ending up stood here, like this.

LENNY stares at his mum. CAROLINE stares back at him, lost.

Or is this just us?

She looks at RAY, who looks to the floor.

Is this what we all want?

LENNY looks at RAY, at CAROLINE. He stares at his mum. And then...

LENNY: Just a sec.

LENNY goes to the door, ushers MIA in.

(*To MIA.*) You didn't meet my mum properly, sorry about that. No one really talks about it but she lost half her brain at birth, keep looking at the floor and you'll be alright...

RAY: *Lenny.*

LENNY: She means well.

RAY: Caz.

CAROLINE: (*Quietly.*) Fuck off.

CAROLINE grabs her brolly, and she goes.

Long long silence. Until...

LENNY: (*To MIA.*) You got my ciggies?

MIA hands a packet of cigarettes to LENNY. He stands in the doorway to the yard, and lights up.

MIA: (*To LENNY.*) Is everything alright?

No answer. MIA waits at LENNY's shoulder, uneasy with the atmosphere. Dazed, RAY resumes his inspection of the wheel on the coffin trolley, administering some oil.

Your mum looks terrible, what's happened?

LENNY: (*Shrugs.*) Some fuck up over a stolen car.

MIA: How?

LENNY: Last night. This Goth prick. I'm taxing him. Him and his bird owed me some notes, so he drives us to the cash point, police see us, turns out the girl's fourteen and she's been missing for the last two weeks. They drag us back to the station, and I ring my dad, get him down.

RAY: Make sure he gives you the full facts love.

LENNY: She's not... /

RAY: ie. The Goth prick was admitted to the walk-in centre... /

LENNY: She's not that interested.

RAY: ... with cuts, bruised testicles, and cigarette burns on his hand, and the fourteen-year-old girl wouldn't speak for fear of recriminations.

LENNY: These things happen. And my old lady decides to come down too, on top of everything else now she thinks I'm a kiddy fiddler, you know what I'm saying?! She's spitting feathers, he's giving it back, 'It's not like that, calm down' and top it all fucking duty solicitor wangles me bail! My mum hits the roof, tells the custody sergeant he needs to keep me locked up for fuck's sake, he threatens to lift her for breach of the peace, she tells him to fuck off, and he nicks her. Bang. Two hours later, Goth prick and his old man put two bricks through the front window, glass everywhere, my mum's cut. It's fucking... They're out of order, you know what I'm saying?

He stops, smiling at it all, but lost, not amused.

Anyway.

LENNY stubs out his cigarette, and moves inside.

RAY: (*To MIA.*) See you again maybe.

LENNY: Are you off?

RAY looks at LENNY, edges past him, and goes.

MIA: Bye.

RAY has left his cigarettes on the coffin. He stops in the doorway, his back to LENNY and MIA. In the time it takes to tap his pockets, realise, and turn back into the room, MIA has gone to LENNY and enveloped him in a fierce and passionate kiss. RAY stops, embarassed as their kiss nears its end and steps outside, so he's mostly out, a litle bit in, hidden by the door jamb and the door left ajar.

(*To LENNY.*) Better?

LENNY nods, their foreheads touching.

Me and you, that's all Len, yeah?

LENNY offers a smile.

I'm sorry about your mum.

LENNY: It's a fuck up.

MIA: Come here… Don't worry, you've got me. We've got each other.

She kisses him again.

I wanted to show you. (*She takes some paper from her pocket.*) You know what we've been talking about…?

He breaks away.

What?

LENNY: Head's pounding.

MIA: Come here.

LENNY: I thought I'd told you.

MIA: You did.

LENNY: So why you bringing it up again? All this talk, it's fucking… You either belong here, or you don't, you know what I'm saying? / Can't have it both ways.

MIA: And I've told you, I *don't* belong here, cos *here's* the town Len, it's skag, it's sniff, it's every corner. And that's not… I can't do that any more.

LENNY: I know you can't…

MIA: I can't sleep. I wake up, I feel shit… It's just a buzz, that's all it is, *it's horrible fucking stuff,* and that's why I'm jacking it in, that's why I want you to come with me.

Beat.

LENNY: (*Of the piece of paper.*) What is it?

MIA: Read it.

LENNY: *I don't wanna read it.*

MIA: You're acting like a stuck up kid.

LENNY: Give it / here…

He grabs the paper from her, she grabs it back.

MIA: You're upset, / you're just…

He pulls it free, screws up the piece of paper.

LENNY: Dreaming. Don't go dreaming you can be anything else, not when you take that shit.

MIA: *You're the one give it me.*

LENNY: I know, because you asked. Why'd you go asking?

MIA: I…

LENNY: Your brothers, your dad, getting in your hair, blah, blah, got your Saturday job, doing your B-Tec, and it's small town boredom, you know what I'm saying? Not very original, but it's you, yeah? *You* took the drugs, *your* own choice, and now it's like I'm causing the problem. All this grief I'm getting, all this talk. I want to get back to being us again. Few more weeks, I'll get the last bit of cash together, and I'm going to put down a deposit.

MIA: For what?

LENNY: You're not the only one dreaming. Been putting stuff away. All those new apartments going up by the river, they're townhouses, they're fucking A-list. They want the new breed, don't want Tesco workers, don't want Phones 4 U, do they? They want people who aren't gonna sit around watching the world go by. It's not like I don't appreciate what you're saying. I see it.

He takes a wrap of cocaine from his pocket.

But you're *in*, yeah? And so you're looking down. Yeah?

Climb as high as you can go, you don't need no leaving. You're above, so why do you need out? Town can't get up this high, not up where you are.

He offers her the wrap.

I'll look after you.

Beat.

MIA: *No.*

He throws the wrap at her.

LENNY: *Well then fuck off on / your own!!!*

MIA: *YOU fuck off… I don't want to go on my own!!!*

MIA pulls up, holding her arm gingerly. Silence. MIA sits. LENNY watches her.

LENNY: (*Of her arm.*) You sure that's not bust?

No answer.

Told you to get it looked at didn't I?

MIA: 'I bumped into a door.'

LENNY: 'I got lippy.'

MIA: Is that why you hit me? Cos I've got a tongue in my head? I'm not your mum.

LENNY: Never said you were.

MIA: Don't take it out on me.

LENNY: I lashed out. I told you. I do shit I don't understand, always have. See me collecting flies, I'm a kid, got my flies for my fishing, show them to the other kids and they're laughing, 'What you collecting flies for wanker?' I like the flies, they're beautiful colours. But then I put the flies away, and I go out and I do shit to people that other people don't have the bollocks for. I know it's bad, but I feel good. If I

57

hit you again I'll say I'm sorry, or I'll get nicked, either way I don't care.

MIA: But you won't hit me again. Not when you're calm. (*Beat.*) Not when *I'm* calm.

LENNY: (*Wry.*) You reckon?

MIA: (*Of the wrap on the floor.*) All I've got in my head is coke… What do I do to get it out…?… Eh? Why'd I ever start it?… Len…

She gets the screwed up piece of paper, smoothing it out as she speaks.

My dad thinks I'm going to college, you know how mental he'd be if he knew I was seeing you…? Do you know what it feels like, lying to him all the time? (*Of the paper.*) So just read it. Please. I printed it off… We get a train, we just… A plane. A boat. And the places we can go to… We volunteer, to work somewhere. But we can decide what we want to do… I want somewhere we can, somewhere that's not… Maybe like… Africa, or somewhere, or fucking… That's not coke, that's not…

LENNY: Mars.

MIA: Mars, yeah. And where we'd go, we'd just go for a bit, we'd help, but after that we'd leave, we'd keep moving. Len. Always. And we won't ever come back. The world wants us…yeah? It wants us to believe, but we'll tell it we're *ourselves,* that what's in our heads is like, that how life *can* be is in our heads, that *we* thought of it, that…

She stops, breathless. Starts again.

(*Slower.*) I wasn't born to die. Not here. I won't do it. Too many things get missed, it's through the cracks, it's… Five months ago, didn't I decide I was going to fall in love with you? Fuck knows why, but aren't I your saviour? Why are you with me, if you don't want me to save us? (*Beat.*) Len.

LENNY stares at MIA, at the pages of paper, lost in the possibility, in her abandonment.

LENNY: What about me?

MIA: I love you. That's what.

LENNY: I meant my pre-cons, stuff like that.

MIA: We'll think of something?

LENNY: Yeah?

MIA: I promise.

She kisses him. His mobile rings.

Ignore it.

It rings. He looks at the number.

Ignore it.

It rings still, he waits, can't resist.

LENNY: (*Phone.*) Alright?

MIA: Fuck.

LENNY: (*Phone.*) Nothing. / Just Mia.

MIA: *Tell them to fuck off…*

LENNY: (*Phone.*) Yeah?… I don't / know. I'm busy.

MIA: Hang up. *Hang up.*

LENNY: Yeah?… Is it?… Right. Sound. Sound. See you in ten.

He hangs up.

MIA: (*Weary.*) Do you see what you just did?

LENNY: It's a party. Shift a ton of white, and dream about our new place. (*Through a smile.*) You're not going to fucking Africa, alright?

She turns and heads for the exit. LENNY moves quickly, takes her by the wrist.

LENNY: *I told you to stay.* I thought we were together.

MIA: You tell me.

LENNY: We are.

MIA: So prove it.

LENNY: *Prove it how?! Fuck's sake, I dream about / you, I fucking…*

MIA: Not words Lenny…

LENNY: Well that's all you're going to get cos what you're asking, it's fucking… This is the only thing I'm good at, do you know what I'm saying?

Beat.

MIA: Fuck off.

MIA turns to go, LENNY grabs her arm tighter, he takes her other arm.

LENNY: *You're not walking out on me.*

MIA: Watch me.

LENNY: (*Exploding suddenly, grabbing her, shaking her.*) *I said fucking stay!!*

MIA: Get off me…

She pulls her hand free from his. He grabs her again, and she turns and scratches him down the face. RAY steps into the doorway.

RAY: Lenny!

MIA slips free and exits. LENNY makes to follow.

LENNY: I fucking / told you!

RAY: Let her go…

LENNY: *I told her…*

RAY: Lenny.

LENNY: *She's not fucking going!!*

RAY: Calm down.

LENNY: *Get the fuck off me!*

> *LENNY exits, following after MIA. As the memory fades the lights change and RAY and LENNY are back in the positions they held before the memory of MIA began.*

RAY: why did you kill her? what she wanted…

LENNY: how do you know what she wanted?

RAY: i heard, i…you shouldn't've killed her. not for that.

LENNY: i didn't kill her.

RAY: you wouldn't be in the shit you / are now if you'd just…

LENNY: if i'd just what? like it's that easy? i'll always be in the shit, dad, yeah? and i've got news, dad, yeah? no point doing what people tell me to, never. no point behaving the way people want me to, *never.* cos other people, they act like they got something i should look up to, and i look, and it's bollocks, you know what i'm saying?

RAY: so why did you go after her?

LENNY: because i'd upset her. i wanted to make things better.

> *LENNY stares at his dad.*

you think i killed her.

> *Beat. RAY grabs the coffin lid.*

what's going on?

> *RAY moves towards LENNY with the lid.*

what about mia?

RAY: she's dead.

LENNY: i don't mean that, i mean what i just told you.

RAY: i've got your word for it. and i've got everyone else's.

LENNY: so believe me. i didn't kill her.

RAY: you don't know how hard it is to believe in a single thing. in anything.

LENNY: you need to believe in your son.

RAY: i want to.

LENNY: so say it.

RAY: what difference does it make?! (*Exploding.*) *it's too late now, you're gone, you're dead len, and that's the point isn't it...you're dead, you're just fucking...!!* (*Calmly.*) come on.

LENNY: what?

RAY: get inside.

LENNY: we're still talking.

RAY: it's not getting us anywhere.

LENNY: that's cos you're not listening. let's go through it again.

RAY: i've heard enough.

LENNY: one more time.

RAY: get in!!

LENNY: (*Climbing into the coffin.*) alright, alright, i'll get in for fuck's sake. but you're not putting the lid on, not yet.

RAY: we'll see about that.

LENNY: no way, no fucking way. i want to see what you're made of.

RAY: you know what i'm made of. / it's not about me len, it's about you.

LENNY: streaky piss. yeah.

RAY: less than that.

LENNY: *much* less, and you're my *dad* for fuck's sake, you're my *DAD!*

RAY: too late now.

LENNY: i've scratched yours, you need to scratch mine.

RAY: bu bum.

LENNY: 'i'm here all week.'

RAY: 'i said, he's here all week.'

LENNY: *no lid dad please.*

RAY: can't

LENNY: *LID!*

RAY: can't.

LENNY: i'll help you get away from mum.

RAY: lie down.

LENNY: did you hear me?

RAY: what?

LENNY: bu bum.

RAY: 'i'm here all week.'

LENNY: get your hammer.

RAY: what?

LENNY: your hammer. when she comes back from the garage, get your hammer. *you're the hammer man aren't you?* get your hammer and hit her.

RAY: you think that's what i want?

LENNY: how many years you worked beside / the dead dad?

RAY: jesus.

LENNY: what man makes a sacrifice like that, to put money in her pocket dad, yeah? solid oak, cut from the tree, and she's never cared what you do.

RAY: *you just can't help yourself can you?!! nasty, malicious bastard!*

CAROLINE: (*Off.*) Ray? *Ray…*

RAY stops as he hears CAROLINE's voice. She sounds frenzied, disturbed, and he goes to the door to the yard, meeting her as she enters.

RAY: Alright?

She pushes past him.

CAROLINE: *No I'm not.*

LENNY: get your hammer.

CAROLINE: (*Pulling at a rip in her pocket.*) Seen what they did to me?

RAY: Who?

CAROLINE: Kids by the crossing.

LENNY: get your hammer.

RAY: i love her, she loves me. where did you learn so much hate?

CAROLINE: Vicious little bastards, they surrounded me…

RAY: Who did?

LENNY: it's easy.

CAROLINE: Spitting at me.

RAY: then do it yourself, eh?!

CAROLINE: Ray.

LENNY: no fucking worries.

RAY: *i thought you said you're not a killer.*

LENNY: i'm not!!

RAY: then stop acting like a fucking moron!!!

CAROLINE: *What are you talking about?*

RAY: Len's been playing up again. (*To LENNY.*) i don't believe this, you're dead and you're still stressing us out.

CAROLINE: What?

RAY: Len's saying he didn't kill the girl. (*To LENNY.*) tell / her what you told me.

CAROLINE: *What do you mean he didn't kill her?*

RAY: He's here, you better talk to him. (*To LENNY.*) tell her how you're innocent.

CAROLINE: *Stop fucking about!*

RAY: Listen to him. He told me, and I don't know, you know? Who knows? I can't tell anymore. (*To LENNY.*) go on.

CAROLINE: (*Like RAY's an idiot.*) There's a bunch of kids out there been having a go at me.

RAY: go on.

LENNY: Mum…?

CAROLINE: Hissing at me, 'you're Lenny's Pope's mum…' 'kick the bitch…'

LENNY: It's me.

CAROLINE: (*Now in tears, shaking.*) Ray.

LENNY: Dad told me to talk to you.

CAROLINE: They ripped my coat.

LENNY: I been thinking.

CAROLINE: I was scared.

LENNY: Nothing else to do, lying in my coffin mum, yeah?

CAROLINE: Ray.

LENNY: And I will.

CAROLINE: Listen to me when I'm talking.

LENNY: Like you wanted.

CAROLINE: *Go and sort them out.*

LENNY: I'll be your boy.

CAROLINE: Ray.

LENNY: Mum.

CAROLINE: *Ray.*

LENNY: I'll be your boy. (*Beat.*) *why won't she look at me?*

CAROLINE: *You bastard! Listen to me!!*

CAROLINE belts RAY across the face, and he lets out a roar of rage.

Grabbing the hammer in retaliation, RAY lunges at CAROLINE, who drops to her knees, shielding herself. RAY has the hammer raised above CAROLINE's head. He stops suddenly, gasping for breath, staring down at her. He drops the hammer, and goes to LENNY.

RAY: (*Soft.*) lie down.

LENNY: please dad. no lid dad, yeah? it's all i'm asking.

RAY eases LENNY down, he lies flat.

RAY: lie down. you're dead.

Long silence. RAY slumps on the side of the coffin.

CAROLINE: You were going to hit me.

He shakes his head.

Why were you going to hit me?

RAY: I wasn't.

CAROLINE: *So what the fucking hell were you doing?!*

RAY is staring at the coffin.

RAY: (*Of the coffin.*) I can't do it… The quality's not there. I'm going to have to ring Brewer. He can get something delivered.

CAROLINE: *Ray.*

RAY: Makes you laugh. Spend all that time making it, and some bastard's going to burn it anyway.

CAROLINE: Tell me.

RAY: *In a minute, I'm trying, I'm… Fuck…* (*RAY breathes.*) Day I started here, Brewer said if I showed some pride I'd be on my way. On my way where? What would he mean by that?

CAROLINE: I've had enough.

RAY: I know you have. *I've had enough myself… (He breathes.)* And the day you found out you were pregnant, I'm thinking, 'This is what he means'.

CAROLINE: *Ray.*

RAY: Because I felt. I was calm. 'She's got me. I've got a job. We love each other.' It was a perfect time. Things were like I'd thought they'd be.

CAROLINE: I'm going.

RAY: (*Raging.*) *You just asked me why I was going to hit you!!*

She stops, stares at him. RAY swallows.

(*Calmer.*) How typical's that? You ask me a question, and you don't listen to the answer.

CAROLINE: I can work it out for myself.

RAY: See my face.

CAROLINE: Leave it.

RAY: It's sour. Some days...

CAROLINE: I'm going.

*He wilts suddenly, like the pressure drops. Everything stops.
She waits.*

Ray.

RAY: *What?... It's a fuck up isn't it!?...*

CAROLINE: Are you...? / What's...?

RAY: *What?... What?* I stare at myself, and it's like I'm
obsessed, this thing, this. *'He* looks the same as me, that
bloke over there, same age, same kind of bloke. Look how
his wife's all over him. Why's he good enough for her?
Why haven't I ever been good enough?' For you... Greedy
face. Me. And I know, because you're who you are.
There's Lenny, there's me, and then there's other...things.
That I don't get to see. So I'm sorry. About the hammer.

CAROLINE: Sorry?

RAY: I think I'm just that kind of a person. (*Gestures outside.*)
You go up that path, at the top of the yard, and look down
the hill into the town. All this re-building. (*Laughs.*) To me,
it's chaos, and being the sort of person I am, for me Caz,
there's some things you can't change.

CAROLINE: I just / want to go home.

RAY: *Some things don't go away...* At such a perfect time, in our
lives, you walked out on me and Lenny.

CAROLINE: Jesus.

RAY: *What? It's a fuck up isn't it...?... You need to listen...*

CAROLINE: No.

LENNY: *Yeah.* Two months old, and he was... And no matter
how much they change all that out there, (*Touches his head.*)
in here, that first time you left, you died. To me. You're my
ghost. *You're* my ghost.

CAROLINE: What?

RAY: (*Laughs.*) I know it's twenty-four years ago, I know I said the *first* time. I said the *first* time, because how many men do you know have had their wife walk out on them five times, and lived to tell the tale? Apart from me. Five times you left. For weeks on end. Where?

CAROLINE gets out her mobile.

Where did you go?… *What the bloody hell are you doing?!*

CAROLINE: I'm calling a cab, / I need to go home…

RAY: *No!*… Five times you left, and five times you… You need to listen to me… 'When she comes back, how long will she stay before she goes again?' Lenny crossing his fingers for good luck, the gossip: 'The fella who works for Brewer. His wife keeps walking out on him.' In the end I'm thinking, 'Why don't you just *fuck off* Caz'. Yeah?

Pause.

So I'm sorry. For the hammer. It's been a bucket of shit. Much of it my fault. I know how you've never done any bad things, really bad things, why should I blame you so much? But I'm just telling you. It's what's been in my head.

She sits. Her resistance fading.

I used to tell Len stories. Saturdays. In the workshop. Jokes, routines. And stories. 'Mum doesn't really want us.' 'Mum promised herself the world, and you've ruined it for her…' 'Let's build the strongest coffin ever, let's put your mum in it. The dead don't come out again Len. It'll just be me and you.'

Pause.

And when you start, it's hard to stop. Caz… Do you see?

CAROLINE: See what? That you hate me?

RAY: (*Laughs.*)

CAROLINE: You don't hate me?

RAY: I was trying... If it sounds like I hate you, then it's...

CAROLINE: It's a slip of the tongue.

RAY: *Caz.*

CAROLINE: So what?

RAY: *Look at me... A fucking hammer Caz.*

CAROLINE: You wanted to kill me.

RAY: *Yes! I did. For a split fucking second.* I did... Half my life, so much fucking anger I can hardly get my breath, and tonight I could've done it... *Really done it...* Lenny told me, 'It's easy'. And I look down, I'm holding the hammer, and it is, it's so easy to let it all just... But you're my wife. And I love you.

Silence. He goes back to the coffin, runs a hand over it.

Anyway, get tomorrow out the way and you'll be hitting the road again, find your 'thing'.

CAROLINE: Will you stop beating me with that bloody stick? Twenty-five years, and you can't think of anything else to say.

No answer.

(*Angry suddenly.*) When I came back, (*Sarcastic.*) that *fifth* time, how old was he? Nine? I told you, didn't I? 'This is us Ray, it's what we've got. I'm staying cos it's not fair on Len.'

RAY: Yeah.

CAROLINE: You remember me saying it?

RAY: More or less.

CAROLINE: Well I *did.* And things were alright. Before Lenny. Not perfect, I don't remember *perfect* Ray. But from the moment he was born I felt... I was... Something changed.

Why do you think it changed? You won't know, so don't try and answer. I couldn't work out where *I* was. *Caroline.* How do you face all that, a kid, the... *I* came first, *I* was here first, and there's got to be room for both of us, otherwise it isn't going to work. The first time I left, I rang you to make sure Len was alright, did you forget that?

RAY: No.

CAROLINE: *No.* The money ran out and I rang you back. Do *ghosts* do that?

RAY: What?

CAROLINE: No. So it wasn't like... I died, not like you described it. The amount of times I left and came back, that's not someone who's dead. I hated myself, and every time I came back it was because of Lenny. Because I loved him. And since he was nine, I've fought tooth and nail for him. I've been here for him.

RAY: I know.

CAROLINE: *So you think it's my fault that kid's lying there now!*

RAY: No.

CAROLINE: *Well you hadn't fucking better.*

RAY: I was just trying to tell you how it's been.

CAROLINE: I know how it's been. Bitter *You felt so fucking sorry for yourself that you ruined it for everyone else...* (*Calmer.*) And we can't have Lenny back... We won't get another chance.

Silence. RAY stares at her. Finally, he turns, and goes to the pass door, and through into the rest of the building.

Now what're you...?

She waits.

RAY returns with a bottle of whisky and two glasses.

RAY: (*Pours a drink.*) Brewer's desk. Special occasions.

CAROLINE: For God's sake.

RAY: Have one.

CAROLINE shakes her head. He sits next to her, pours another. Silence, until…

CAROLINE: What did he offer you?

RAY: He hasn't.

CAROLINE: You'll need some redundancy.

RAY: (*Of the bottle.*) I've got his Glenfiddich.

She takes the glass and has a sip. She hands the glass back.

CAROLINE: You're not just going to roll over.

RAY: I won't.

CAROLINE: Get what you're worth.

RAY: How much is that do you think?

CAROLINE: Find out how much is left on the house, and ask for that. Pay it off.

He looks at her.

RAY: This is what you wanted to talk about.

CAROLINE: I need my share, I…I've saved something, but it won't be enough.

RAY: Sell the house?

CAROLINE: Sat up there on my own, you get a lot of time to think.

RAY: I did ring you.

CAROLINE: I know, it's not criticising, you've been busy with the coffin. But I'm sitting there, and what do you do? You know me Ray, head full of plans, and I was working things out. A bit for you, a bit for me.

RAY: (*Pours another drink.*) For what?

CAROLINE: Now I can do it, I don't know where to start. The amount of days I'm stood there in the shop. 'It won't always be like this'. Shoes all day. 'When there's nothing more you can do for Lenny, think of all the things Caroline's going to do'.

RAY: Like what?

CAROLINE: 'Lenny might join the church.' 'Lenny might meet a girl.' You're not the only one hearing voices. Kept myself going. And saving. Thirty quid a month.

She takes the bottle fom RAY.

Don't have any more you'll be sick.

And now I'm here…

She stops. Waits. RAY moves to her.

RAY: Caz.

CAROLINE: Don't.

RAY: You wanted / to go home.

CAROLINE: *Don't.*

He waits. She covers her face with her hand. Until…

I came down… Why I came down. This evening. After the funeral, I'm going… I'll be gone. Which you're used to, I know you are, but there's no more reasons, after tomorrow, not now Lenny's dead. It's different this time. I won't be coming back… Why would I? Look at us…we're… And I'll need to live, so I wanted to talk, about the house. You might not want to talk about it, but I think we should sell it. You'll be rattling around in there by yourself. (*She stops.*) And I wanted to ask you… I don't know why I should be asking you. But I sat there in the house, today, and I got this thought going on, you're down here, I'm up there, and Lenny used to be in between us. But before Lenny, it was

73

like it was today, you busy down here with your dad, me
up to something or other at home, and then about six, I'd
stroll down and you'd take me for a drink, or we'd go to
'Mr George's' and strut our stuff... Do you remember what
that was like? That's what I was thinking, I know we're
older, and there's the whole thing with Lenny, but where
did it go, that...easiness? Is it something that stays, like you
put it in deep freeze? Or is that it? Like, now it's gone, can
we get it back?

They face each other.

I just want someone to tell me.

She waits. She moves away.

The funeral'll be quick, I thought I'll do a few sandwiches
afterwards.

RAY: I was thinking about that.

CAROLINE: About what?

RAY: Lenny came into the kitchen, and you were making
cheese and pickle. He was in his boxer shorts. He said 'The
Police are outside. I didn't kill the girl. Don't let them take
me.' And we were like, 'Yeah, sure, same old story Len.'
But then you made a pot, and we believed him. You know
how dreams do that? He put the telly on, and there was
a news report. About the girl's death. But it was on the
screen at the same time, in slow motion, and you could see
the girl falling into the road. And Len was trying to save
her. So we all went and stood on the doorstep. We told the
police. 'You've come for the wrong man. This is our son.
You can't have him.' (*He stops. Explains.*) This morning. I
woke up. I tried to get the dream back and carry it on. The
clock went off. I had to get up.

*CAROLINE takes a photograph from her pocket, and lays it on
LENNY's chest. Slowly, she lowers her face so that her cheek
touches LENNY's. She stays there, muttering to her son; a low
mumble of pain.*

RAY watches, broken by the intimacy of the moment.

Finally, CAROLINE kisses LENNY on the cheek and straightens up.

CAROLINE: (*To LENNY.*) See you in the morning son.

She looks back at RAY, and exits.

He waits. He looks at the coffin. He goes suddenly to the door.

RAY: Caz.

We can see him peering across the yard. Has she gone?

RAY steps back inside the room. He looks across at the coffin, unsure of himself, and turns and leaves again.

(*Off.*) *Caz.* I'll give you a lift…

Beat

(*Off.*) Wait for me.

The room is empty, save for the hammer on the floor, the flowers on the table, the coffin, the coffin lid leant at its side, and LENNY's body.

A silence.

End.

cloud:burst

Character

DOMINIC, 30s

The present day

cloud:burst was first performed on 31 October 2005 at the Linbury Studio, Royal Opera House, with the following company:

DOMINIC, Graeme Hawley

Director Chris O'Connell
Producer Julia Negus
Original soundscape Andy Garbi
Set and Costume Design Janet Vaughan
Lighting Design James Farncombe
Technician/Re-lights Will Evans
Stage Manager (London and Bristol) Andy Lawson
Company Stage Manager/on the book (New York City) Lizzie Wiggs
Production Runner (Coventry) Mia Nolan
Design Pixeltrix

It was subsequently toured in the UK and opened on 23 May 2006 at 59E59 Theater, New York, as part of the Brits Off Broadway Season.

Theatre Absolute would like to thank:
Louise Blackwell and Kate McGrath at Fuel, David Jubb at BAC, Alan Rivett and Neil Darlison at Warwick Arts Centre, Coventry, Vince Brosnan at City College, Coventry, Dan Danson at the Tobacco Factory, Bristol, Camilla Whitworth-Jones and The Helen Hamlyn Trust, Coventry City Council, Alison Gagen and Arts Council England, West Midlands, Peter Tear, and Richard Jordan.

GRAEME HAWLEY (Dominic)
Graeme trained at Manchester Metropolitan School of Theatre and he has previously worked with Theatre Absolute on *Raw, Street Trilogy* and with Chris O'Connell on *cloud:burst* as part of the BAC's October Fest in 2004. Graeme is also a founder member of Manchester-based Homegrown theatre company and his work with them includes *Traffic and Weather* and *Hidden Markings,* for which he won the MEN Most Promising Newcomer award in 2000. Other theatre credits include: *Love and Money* (Royal Exchange, Manchester/Young Vic), *Romeo and Juliet* (Eye), *Measure for Measure, Schweyk* and *Howie the Rookie* (Library Theatre, Manchester) and *Little Malcolm* (Octagon Theatre, Bolton). His TV credits include *Emmerdale, The Royal, Cops, A & E, Strumpet, Touch of Frost, The Forsyth Saga, Born and Bred, Heartbeat, Shameless* and *Big Night Out.* Graeme has also worked extensively with BBC Radio 4 drama.

DOMINIC waits as the audience file in. Alone in the space, he can watch them. The lights change…

DOMINIC: Shaking, ten thousand feet, rays, hit. Eyes.
Look down. See. Jigsaw of emotion. Hope.
Of myself.
Cloud. Burst.

Music grows, building to a cacophony of sound, on and on, on and on, on and on. Finally, the music breaks, and levels.

Morning.
Signal comes, and OB trucks, satellite discs, away. Dust stream, up. 90 mph, willing it. I drive down the street. Storm, of cloudburst. Other side: out. Roads, black tongues, lick, away. I'm driving. Driven. Cloudburst. OB trucks, satellite discs, gone. Dust stream, up. Street, falls; it's quiet.
All knowledge, with no warning, has been given to me, and to my wife: so we understand: the way. Of things.
Cloudburst, I'm the only father in the world who feels this way.
Sit, read; papers.
Sit, read. And again tomorrow. And again, tomorrow.
But no more headlines; of my family, my child.
Cloud:Burst.
Why my child?

He breathes. Until…

Listen. This house.

He moves through the physical space of the house.

Room.
To.

Room.

To.

Room.

To.

Room.

Memories. Our life. Natalie's life. Yeah? A visit has been, and the visit is. Gone. How can things ever be normal? I'm alone, and together, and apart, eight weeks caged in this fucking cloudburst, where people want and people just.

'Dominic we want to do an article for the Sunday edition.'

'Dominic, tell us how you feel about the murderer.'

'It's eleven at night'.

'Yes. Sorry. But Dominic, can you speak?'

And people just. Well, so do I sleep? Do I wake? Do I stay in, do I go out? Faces, ghosting up the drive. Two, four. Doorbell. Questions. More stories, columns, exclusives. And so I won't go, out. I won't eat, not now. And they wait. Outside. Tents. Outside. Broadcast. Trucks, rain, the dark, and the night. Lights, glow. How can this street, sleep? Eight weeks, and now they're gone. Bradshaw, arrested, no more interviews, no more need, but in this burst, I still need to, I still need…(*Silence.*) To what?

He dials on his mobile.

Helen, it's Dominic Thorpe. I was wondering, can we go for a drink?

Yeah. Sandra? She's sleeping. She won't speak to me. Yeah. That'd be good. I'll see you there. Bye.

He hangs up. DOMINIC *calls upstairs.*

Sandra…? I was talking to Helen from the newspaper. (*No answer.*) Sandra, that was Helen on the phone. I'm going for a drink with her.

No answer. He waits, disturbed by Sandra's refusal to talk. Shaking it away, he walks towards Helen.

'Hiya.'

Like the way Helen talks. Last eight weeks, she writes, my story.

'Hiya Dom. Are you okay?'

'No. But let's just have a drink. What do you want?'

'Erm, a lager shandy please.'

To the barman.

'A lager shandy, and a bitter mate.'

He turns back to Helen.

'I've got a story for you.'

'Dom,' Helen says. 'I thought we'd talked about this. The paper won't do any more stories, not at the moment.'

'No, listen. I went back to work, and it was a fucking disaster.'

'Really?'

'Yeah. The phone was ringing, and I couldn't answer it. I work in a call centre for fuck's sake. So what, my kid's just been murdered. I'm taking it out on the shareholders, do you know what I mean? Let their profits shrink. Write an article on that.'

'On what?'

'That. I want you to write another article on me. Then I want you to write another one. And then another. You guys, all this attention, you've made me feel…'

'Feel what?'

'That I. I… Okay, no more press conferences, no more TV, but the story is…You know? This story's still going on… It's… I… How I feel… If you all just piss off, like when the OB trucks left last week, no one told me they were going. If it's like no one's bothered anymore, then. Helen, this story's not over because I still want to, I still want to say…'

Beat.

'Say what?'

He stares at her. Swallows.

'It doesn't matter.'

She, turns.

'Did I tell you?' I say. 'We got a letter. From Bradshaw's parents.'

DOMINIC looks back to the audience, moves to them, and recites the letter.

'Dear Mr Thorpe,

We have seen and we have watched your face for weeks on end, staring out at us on the news, and in the papers. You've been brave, and dignified in the way you've supported your wife, and the memory of what our son did to your child is something we can't forget. If you and your wife can find it within you to meet us, and let us know that in some small way we can be forgiven for the pain our son has brought upon your family, we will be always grateful.

Yours, Mr and Mrs Andrew Bradshaw.'

Burst.

Music blasts in. A club. He dances to the music. Wild.

One, two, three, four, five, six. Fifteen, that many. Twenty, twenty one!

We finish at the pub, and Helen takes me dancing.

I've got.

I need.

Helen takes me dancing, because she knows.

Helen takes me dancing, because I might explode.

Helen takes me dancing, because she knows I have to be.

Eyes, peeling, me, off.

'It's him, it's that Dominic. He's that bloke whose kid was murdered.'

Peeling, eyes. All, eyes. Doesn't everyone know, me.

DOMINIC keeps dancing, until the music slows, his movements start to halt, and finally he is still, on his knees, his head on the kitchen tiles in his house.

Until…

I'm called the casual, man. Dom never worries, about life. Apparently. Who the fuck doesn't worry. About life. But, here I am. Believe it, yeah? Me, the smiler. Can't deny it: all my life, the good times. And dad: 'Do you think you should drink so much?' Mum: 'Do you think you should sunbathe so much?' Sandra: 'Wake up Dom, life's for living.' 'Dom, did you put the washing out?' 'Dom, did you apply for a new job?' 'Dom, do you want to make cold calls all your life?' Yes, I know. Yes, I did. No, I don't. And one day, I'll be, something. This time, in a year, in two. Just. So, hush. Yeah?

DOMINIC takes a bunch of knives and forks, drying them in a rhythm; the routine of a life lost.

Family has to live, without. No fear. We did. Regular. Natalie wakes, we sleep, she watches TV. Sandy wakes, they eat, brekkie. I wake. I take Nat, to school. We just: we eat, we drive, we drop off, we pick up, we laugh, we dance, we jive, we eat, again, we wash, we kiss, and we, sleep. A way, to live. Just…

He smiles. Whispers

'There. is. no. fucking. bogey. man. out. there.'
What? Naive?

Suddenly…

Raaaaaaa! Angry people, TEN O'CLOCK NEWS!! STATISTICS, angry voices. 'The world's a black hole!!' (*He smiles.*) No. World is shining. Gleaming.

He turns upstage, stops. His denial wrenched from him…

'THERE IS NO FUCKING BOGEY MAN OUT THERE!!!'

He looks to the audience. Breathes. Continues…

That morning; Saturday. And in the kitchen, Natalie's smiling.

'What you eating?' I ask her.

She giggles.

'What you eating you cheeky bugger.'

'A chocolate…'

She laughs. We chase. I, chase her. To the end of the garden.

'Don't go far!'

I call.

'Dad. It's only three streets away.'

'Your mum said.'

'Where is she?'

'Shopping.'

'When's she back?'

'Later'

'Is she getting my birthday pressie?'

'I don't know.'

'Can I have some money?'

'Are you going or not?

He digs into his pocket, sorting money.

'Come on then, quickly. My film's starting.'

'I'm going to Selina's then, okay?' she says.

He hands over some money.

'Here. Well go on then.'

'Byyyyye!!'

She, calls.

He sits, the sun starts to dip. DOMINIC settles in, rolling a spliff, smoking, watching the film, the sounds of the TV familiar and comforting. Until he sleeps.

Silence. DOMINIC wakes suddenly, startled from his sleep. Looks at his watch. He goes to the end of the garden.

'Nat?… Natalie?!' (*He waits. He does the special whistle he and Natalie share. Nothing.*) 'Natalie?' (*He does the whistle again.*) 'Nat?'

He grabs his mobile, dials:

'Sandra, Nat's not with you is she?'
'Why would she be with me?' Sandra asks.
'I dunno.'
'Fuck's sake Dom, where is she then if she's not with you?'
'She went out to play.'
'Where?… Where's she playing?'
'Erm Selina's, I'm not sure.'
'Dom, I told you she musn't go that far.'
'She's okay. Calm down.' (*Beat.*) 'She'll be fine.'

Blackout.

Lights up.
DOMINIC is kneeling on the floor again, as before, his head on the kitchen tiles.

Thin.
This light.
Quite nice actually, just.
Head. On the tiles.
Sweat. And dried out.
Here.

He rolls onto his back, stares at the ceiling. He hears the sound of feet coming down the stairs.

That'll be Sandra.
Look at the state of me.
Here, we go.
Wife, on fire.

He stands, looks at Sandra.

'Hi-ya. Sandra, not now alright...? My head hurts, I'm fucked.'

'Why didn't you come home last night? You didn't even ring.'

'I know.'

'Why the fuck are you behaving like this?'

'For Christ's sake Sandy, why do you THINK? Have you got any idea what's been going on around us. Shutting yourself away up there, refusing to talk. I've had to deal with everything, papers, police, interviews.'

'Yeah, well aren't you the big hero.'

'What does that mean?'

'You know what it means.'

'No, come on, now we're getting somewhere, speak to me, spit it out yeah? Tell me what you think of me. I need to know what you're thinking!!'

'I think, you should stop chasing the papers; it makes us look sick, people get the wrong idea.'

'So let them. We didn't start this, Bradshaw killed our kid, what do you expect me to do. Now his parents want to meet us, the letter... You think we can just walk away from that?'

'Yes.'

DOMINIC laughs in her face.

'Well I can't, it's not that easy, I... I need... I... Helen's waiting, she says if we agree to meet the parents, then she needs to know. Helen respects me. We get on. She'll help us through it.'

'I'm not meeting anyone. I'm not saying anything you fucking freak. Helen only "respects" you because our daughter died, it's not you Dom, she doesn't respect you, why the fuck would she?'

He stares at her, crushed.

'Well I'll go by myself then.'

'No.'

Grabbing.
Pushing.
She, grabs.
I, push.
'I will go. I will go.'
'Oh, will you?'
'Yeah. I have to. You, have to. You, me, we have to.'
'Why?'
'This, is, not, the, end.'
'Dominic…'
'This, is, not, the, end. This, is, not, the end. This, cannot,
be, the end.
This.
This.
This.
Grabbing. Pushing.
This.
This.
This.
She, grabs. I, push.
This. This. This…

He swings his fist.

Blood.

He stops.

Spots.

Silence.

Christ.
Soft, crush. Her arse. Sandra's arse, the shape, of an apple.
Soft. Her skin, crushing as she sits, on the chair, by the
window. Hear, her, she's weeping. Lip.
'Get out.'
Cut.

'Get out.'

Silence.
Lights down.

Lights up.
The sound of a car, and the road passing beneath its wheels. A radio plays, the frequency is cracked by the surrounding hills. Derbyshire.

Buxton. Baby's born every two hours in Buxton. And Bakewell. Cakes are baked, in Bakewell. Mum. My Dad. Driving. White lines, on black tongues. I don't speak. Haven't spoken since Sandra. Just, and tired.
'Here son. This is where you need to be. You can't let this tear you both apart. Here,' Dad says, glancing in the mirror, 'is where you can stay, until you're better, and then you need to go home.'
I'm staring at the white, on the tongues.
House.
My old, room.
'Alright then?' dad says, 'Dom, you've got to get your chin up son.'
Dad, while he lights his ciggie, his hand on the bedroom door. Dad's got factory hands. Lathe hands. Used to build the country, hands. Fingers, bones, muscles. Hands to raise, a child.

He stares at his own hands.

In these. What good? For hitting.
Wives.

DOMINIC turns out the light.

Night.

Silence.

Garden.

Sounds of the night. A dog barking, cars passing. DOMINIC takes out his mobile, rings Sandra. Their answer machine is heard:

MACHINE: 'This is Dom and Sandy, we're not here at the moment, please leave a message after the tone.'

DOMINIC holds the phone to his ear, waiting, waiting. He cannot speak, and finally, he hangs up, lowering to the floor where he lies on the grass.

Silence, until…

DOMINIC: Rain.

A light grows at the end of the garden, illuminating a pair of children's wellington boots. He sees the boots, entranced, unsure if they're real, or not. He crawls towards them. Touches them, picks at the mud on one of the boots.

I know this mud, three months ago; a weekend visit and Nat and me, walkers, set loose by grandad. And we did. We walked.

He is on his feet.

Hills. Peaks.
Ditches. And rising, rocked, crags.
Green in brown.
Mud!
To the top of the hill. (*He stares.*) I can see. That's us now. See? And Natalie, asking me about the sky, the sun. About clouds.
'You know clouds right dad?'
'Of course I know clouds. I'm a cloud expert.'
She, laughs.
'How high are clouds?'
'Ten thousand feet.'
'How many are there? Let's count. Dad. Come on. One, two, three, four, five, six, fifteen, that many, twenty, twenty-one. I'm having that cloud over there,' she says.
'Okay.'

'And I know what clouds do dad. They store fantastic things, right down, deep, tucked away, right at the bottom, in the corner.'

'What sort of things?'

'Dreams. Don't let my cloud burst, will you dad?'

'No chance.'

'Promise me.'

'I won't.'

He stops. He looks down at the boots. Moves away, boiling with rage, the music growing.

Kitchen.

Dad's keys.

'What're you doing son?!' dad shouts.

'Where are they?'

'Where's what? What's going on? It's four in the bloody morning!!'

'What's happening to me... Dad... Where's your car keys? I need, I need to... Give me your keys...'

'Dom.'

'Give me your fucking keys!!'

By now the music is flatlining, a howl of feedback.

Roads, black tongues, lick, away. I'm driving. Driven. Helen!...

Ten thousand!

Helen!!

Dad's car, through the night, to Helen's paper. Climb the wall. I look, into the offices.

Now he's climbed the wall, he calls again:

Helen!

She comes out.

'What are you doing here Dom?'

'I need to talk, to, I was in Buxton. At my, and I...'

'Dom.'

'I can't go on any more. I need to get things straight. This
is the story, this…'

'What is?…'

'*Me!* Do the headline Helen, write it. Natalie's dad is…'

'What?'

'When Natalie, when she went.'

He breathes. Starts again.

'When Natalie went out to play, on the day, I only had
to… Words, Helen, I only had to say: you can't go that far,
mum says it's not allowed. Can't you see? I'm the one…
And I've lost both of them. Sandra won't speak, about.
Why? If you did what I did then I'd scream, I'd BLAME
you. Yeah? But she. Nothing. And the way she looks at me.
I can't stand it, people need to know. Natalie died because
I didn't protect her. That's your story, that's why this story
isn't…Write it. Make sure everyone knows.'

And hands, reaching.

'Come down lad.'

Lad? Me? I'm thirty-five, prick. Work, mortgage. And, kid.

'What's your name lad? Can you tell us your name?'

'You know my fucking…Everyone knows who I am…'

'Okay, we're coming up.'

'NO! FUCK YOU!!!!! Keep away, get your fucking, hands
off!!…Hey!

HEY!!! It's okay…they won't tell my story!!!!'

Suddenly, he falls from the wall.
Lights down.

Lights up.
Silence. DOMINIC is in hospital. A machine bleeps. Music plays
softly, and the distant, dreamy sound of a child can be heard,
humming a melody of unspeakable beauty, somewhere near to.
He lifts his eyes.
The song continues. He listens. Until…

A, child.

He listens again. The bleeping of his pulse, and the child's song, rhythmic, hypnotic. Until…

Sandra. She stares. My broken, my leg.
'You're above the children's ward,' she says.
Cloud.
Burst.
And that makes me…
I want to…

He puts a hand over his eyes.

'Go on. Cry,' Sandra says. 'Before you kill yourself.' (*Beat.*) 'And then come home. I can't watch you do this. You're a loser Dom, I've nearly divorced you I don't how many times. Okay? And I blame you, if that's what you want to hear. Part of me hates you for neglecting our little girl. The world is a cruel and dangerous place, and you forgot. You should have accepted that. Long ago. I don't know if there's enough between the two of us; maybe without Nat there's no reason any more. But you're not, guilty.'

Silence.

'Dom?'

Silence.

Burst.

The distant voice of the child rises, the beautiful melody, drifting across the space, and DOMINIC lets the tears flow. Music plays.
Blackout.

Lights up.
DOMINIC dries the knives and forks.

Trial starts. Next month. See, Bradshaw. See, faces. The papers. They'll ask. They'll want, again. Helen rang. Two weeks ago. She wanted to talk. I said, so talk. Ask me. Ask you what? she said. I don't know, just ask me what I've been doing since I fell off that wall. Ask me if I'm going to be available for a whole new bunch of interviews, about the trial, about life, after Nat. Ask me if I'll mind building up to it all again, and then ask me about those two kids murdered last month, ask me if I'm curious why no one spent eight weeks writing about them. (*Smiles.*) Helen, just ASK me. I understand; because now, it's story time. Again.

He regards the audience.

Sunday.
Today.
I like Sundays.
'Sandra?'

He waits.

'Yes.'
'It's Sunday.'
'I know.'
She's in the garden.
'Didn't we always have family dinners, on a Sunday?'
'Yes.'
'I like Sundays.'
'So do I.'
She, calls.

He realises he has dried a third set of knives and forks, smiles to himself, and puts them away.

I've been.

He gets a notebook.

A diary. Just. A few words. To help.
It's…

He looks at the audience, and walks beyond the lights to face them. He reads from the notebook:

'DAY ONE. 24th July. The sun was shining. I remember being excited that one of my favourite films was on the TV that afternoon. The world was a gleaming shining peach, and Natalie was in the kitchen, her hair was braided, her feet, loose in sandals. It was her tenth birthday, and my wife had gone early into town. Me and Nat laughed, and we joked, and she was eating my chocolate. She was always eating my chocolate! We loved each other, and I remember that even though I was impatient to watch the film, I remember thinking how much I loved her, and how much she loved me, as she laughed, and went out of the garden gate…'

He looks at the notebook. At the audience. He closes the notebook.

Cloud.
Life,
Burst.
Begins.

End.